IRISH MUSIC FOR FIDDLE
MADE EASY
BY PHILIP JOHN BERTHOUD

Online Audio   www.melbay.com/21354BCDEB

Audio Contents

1 Factory Girl	16 The Butterfly
2 Paddy's Green Shamrock Shore	17 The Rocky Road to Dublin
3 Planxty Irwin	18 The Rakes of Westmeath
4 Carolan's Dream	19 The Irish Washerwoman
5 The Parting of Friends	20 Caliope House
6 The Derry Air	21 The Cliffs of Moher
7 The Star of the County Down	22 Sergeant Early's Jig
8 Whiskey in the Jar	23 The Jolly Beggarman
9 Oh! The Britches Full of Stitches	24 The Rights of Man
10 John Ryan's	25 The Wren Hornpipe
11 Kerry Polka	26 The Boys of Malin
12 The Rakes of Mallow	27 Miss McLeod's Reel
13 The Road to Lisdoonvarna	28 The Merry Blacksmith
14 Tatter the Road	29 The Star of Munster
15 The Runaway Jig	

1 2 3 4 5 6 7 8 9 0

Visit us on the Web at www.melbay.com — E-mail us at email@melbay.com

Table of Contents

Introduction

This book and recording contains a selection of 29 traditional Irish tunes. They are arranged for easy fiddle, roughly in order of difficulty. The music is clear and easy to read, with all bow directions given. All the music is in first position. Each tune is featured on the accompanying recording, played through at a slow tempo 2 or 3 times.

When working on a particular tune, spend time listening to the recording, in order to familiarize yourself with the sound of the tune. With traditional music, a great deal is picked up by ear. Have the tune going round in your head before attempting to play it. This will make the process more natural and rewarding.

On the recording, each new tune will be "tapped-in" so that you know when the music will start. Aim to play along with the recording as soon as you know a tune well. They are all recorded quite slowly so as to make playing along more manageable.

With traditional Irish music it is quite normal to play a particular tune more than once. In some of the tunes in this book you will find a final note/notes printed in brackets – these notes are designed to be left out when playing a tune for the last time. They are only played if you are going to go back to the beginning of a tune and repeat it. Likewise, some tunes are shown with a single note at the end that is clearly marked to be played the last time through.

Below is an effective plan of action for tackling each new tune:

1. Listen to the tune on the recording a couple of times.

2. Listen to the tune again, this time following the corresponding music in the book.

3. Look more carefully at the music and make sure you understand what you need to do to play it.

4. Now, working at your own pace, begin to play the tune. How slow or fast you go is not important. What is important is that you take care to play the right notes.

5. Check the recording to hear what it should sound like.

6. Keep practicing the tune, getting to know it better.

7. When you are at the stage that you can play the tune from beginning to end, you could try playing along with the recording. If you don't get to the end, don't worry. Set yourself targets such as reaching the end of the first line, then the second line of music.

8. When you know it well, see how much you can play by memory. Some players do this more naturally than others.

Thanks to Dave Wade for mixing and mastering the recording.

Factory Girl

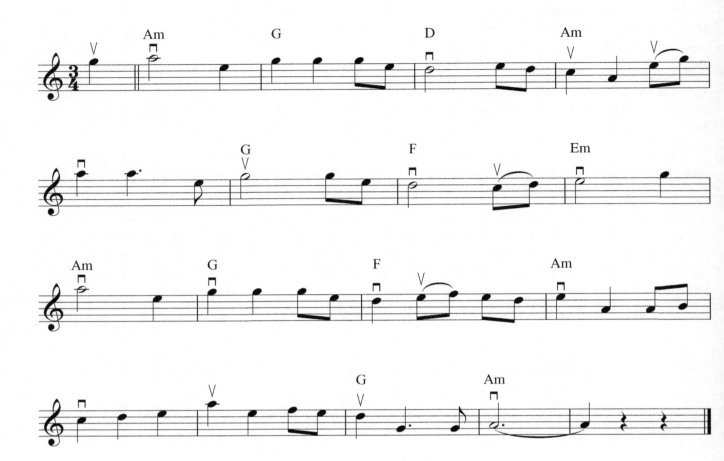

Paddy's Green Shamrock Shore

Planxty Irwin

Carolan's Dream

tr. 5

The Parting of Friends

The Derry Air

The Star of the County Down

Whiskey in the Jar

The Britches Full of Stitches

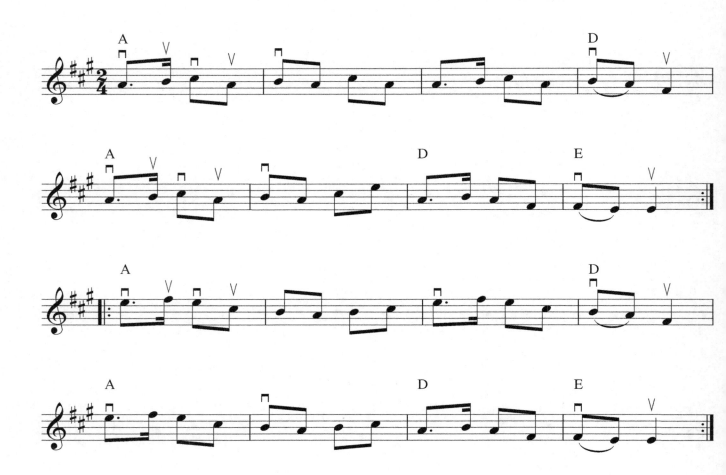

John Ryan's Polka

Kerry Polka

The Rakes of Mallow

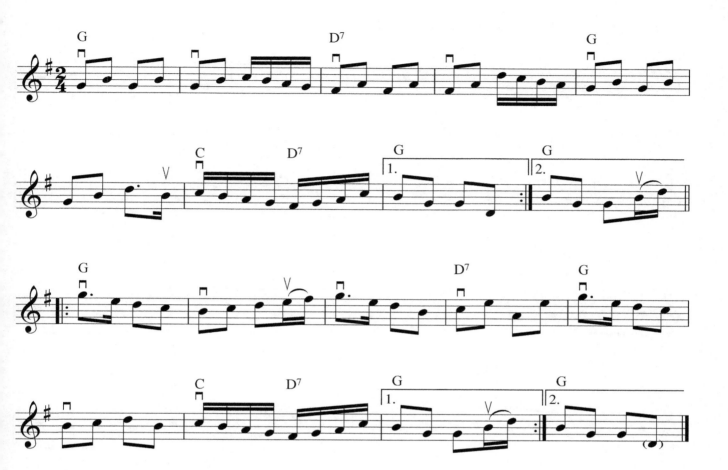

The Road to Lisdoonvarna

Tatter the Road

The Runaway Jig

The Butterfly

The Rocky Road to Dublin

tr. 18

The Rakes of Westmeath

last time only

The Irish Washerwoman

Caliope House

The Cliffs of Moher

Sergeant Early's Jig

The Jolly Beggarman

The Rights of Man

The Wren Hornpipe

The Boys of Malin

Miss McLeod's Reel

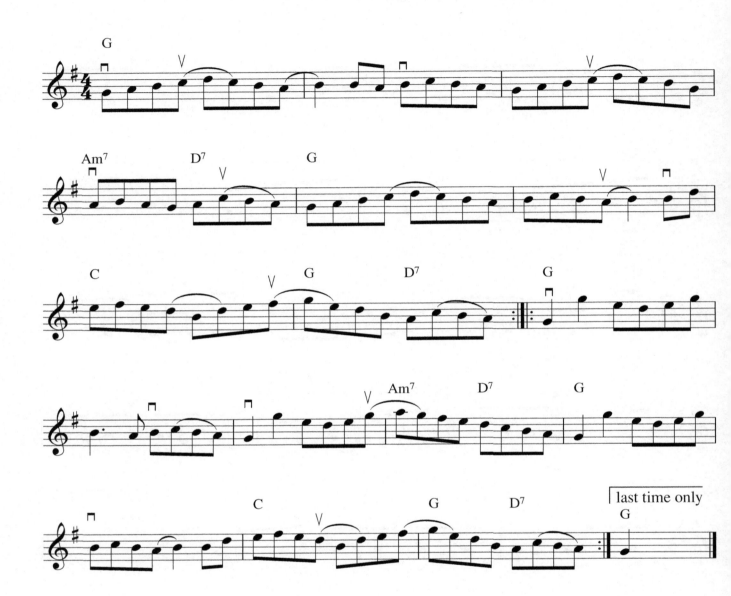

30

The Merry Blacksmith

The Star of Munster

Printed in Great Britain
by Amazon

39248600R00020